Reviews for *That Bo*

A totally delightful, ener~~gent~~ ~~and imaginative~~ ~~book. For~~
lovers of the ancient world, young and old!

Ursula Dubosarsky, Author of over 50 books
and Australian Children's Laureate 2020-2021

*Whenever Terry and I take our time-travelling rubbish
bin for a spin through the ancient mythical lands of
Greece or Midgard, we always take David Conley as our
guide- and if he's not available then we take one of his
books. He's the most knowledgeable expert on Greek
and Norse mythological figures we've ever met, and we've
met them all!*

Andy Griffiths, author of over 30 books
including the critically acclaimed Treehouse
series

Raaaaaaaaaaaaaaaaaa!!!

Apophis, giant snake monster that wants to eat
the Sun.

Some of the best books I have read and very funny.

Aaron, 8

David Conley is a bigger legend than Odin and a bigger marvel than Marvel! He puts the Rock into Ragnarök and the Norse into Norsænivegavinnuverkfæraskúrinngullhringur!!!! This is how the Greeks would have illustrated their myths and legends and it's what the Norse gods really looked like! Trust me, I've asked them.

I loved reading his mythologies - though I had to build a wooden horse and hide inside it to sneak into my son's room to get the books off him to read them.

Dr Craig Cormick OAM, award-winning author of over 40 books for the young and young at heart.

Reading this book just made me want to kill all the humans all over again.

Sekhmet, daughter of Ra

I like all the short stories... I really like it... I never want to stop reading it... I just want to read it forever... it's really good.

Harry, 5

Definitely my favourite book that I've read then read again... Mum when is the next book out?

Will, 7

Your books are the best! I read them over and over, Mum says they are value for money. Your drawings have so much detail and the characters seem so alive (even though some are actually dead). I love learning about mythology and I can even pronounce all the titans and gods names better than my Dad (and spell them correctly too).

Josh, 8

Don't write down that snake trick! Ra's going to see it and know it was me!

Isis, Mother of Horus

It was Isis's plan all along?!?!

Ra, God of the Sun

Told you.

Isis, Mother of Horus

That David Conley is a fantastic writer. All families should have his books. They're perfect for anyone aged 5 to 2 761 years, or when they die, whichever comes first.

Giselle, 12

As a teacher librarian, I am always looking for ways to engage students in reading and even reading about non-fiction topics. Ever since I have had David's books in the library, well they are never really in the library because they are always loaned out. What can I say? Children are really drawn to the imaginative ways these books are presented.

Marion, Teacher Librarian

There's no better feedback for this book then seeing a contented 7 year old boy curled up on the couch engrossed in the hilarious illustrations and intriguing tales. In his words the book is 'very unusual and very interesting'. In my words it's a unique, colourful and irreverent spin on some very old stories. He turns dusty into dazzling. I don't know many Greek myths, and I blame my misfortune on being born before David was sharing his talent with the world!

Emma, Playwright

I'm not that dangerous anymore. Nowadays whenever I want to chop someone up into pieces I just knit myself some socks. I currently have 24 million pairs of socks.

Set, God of Chaos

Dedicated to my three favourite people.

First published 2023

Copyright David Conley 2023.

The moral rights of the creator have been asserted

Dedicated to my three favourite people.

That Book About Egyptian Mythology

David Conley

Contents

The Start Of The World

First it was dark and there was lots and lots of water.

That Book About Egyptian Mythology

In the water, there were three huge snake monsters swimming around...

The Start Of The World

As well as eight gods in a group called the Ogdoad...

The four male gods were Nu, Huh, Kek and Amun. They all looked like frogs.

The goddesses were Naunet, Hauhet, Kauket and Amaunet. They were snakes.

That Book About Egyptian Mythology

Eventually the god Amun sat up...

Took the shape of a man...

The Start Of The World

And let out a big breath...

His breath moved over the waters...

And caused a small mound of earth to form...

The small mound became a big mound called a ben-ben.

The Start Of The World

A lotus flower grew out of the ben-ben.

And a god grew out of the lotus flower.
His name was Ra.

Ra Makes Lots Of Things

Ra made the Sun...

And replaced the darkness with light.

Ra Makes Lots Of Things

And then a whole world formed.

Ra made two gods- Shu and Tefnut.

Shu was God of the Air.

And Tefnut was Goddess of Water.

Ra Makes Lots Of Things

Shu and Tefnut had two kids: Geb and Nut.

Geb grew up to be God of the Earth...

Nut grew up to be Goddess of the Sky...

Next Ra said some magical words....

And a whole bunch of animals popped up out of nowhere.

Ra Makes Lots Of Things

Looking out at everything made Ra get a bit weepy and he had a little cry.

His tears fell to the ground...

And became humans.

From then on there was a world and it had lots of life in it.

Soon two more gods appeared. They were Khonsu and Thoth.

Khonsu was the god in charge of this new thing called the Moon.

And Thoth was really, really clever.

Ra was happy with Thoth and Khonsu...

But he wasn't happy about Geb and Nut...

Ra knew that they would have kids and one of those kids would take his job.

He told them not to have a kid on any day.

That Book About Egyptian Mythology

Geb and Nut really wanted some kids...

So they told Thoth their problem.

And he came up with a plan.

The Ennead

Thoth found Khonsu...

And challenged him to a dice rolling game.

Khonsu agreed, the gods played...

That Book About Egyptian Mythology

And Thoth won.

For his winnings, he claimed five beams of moon light for his prize.

22

The Ennead

Thoth used magic on the moon beams...

Turned each moon beam into a day...

And gave the world five extra days.

Geb and Nut used the extra days to make their kids Osiris, Isis, Set and Nepthys.

Eventually, the kids grew up into gods...

Osiris became the God of Fertility.

The Ennead

Isis became Goddess of Magic.

Nephthys became Goddess of Burials.

And Set became God of Chaos.

Ra didn't seem to mind the gods once they had already been born.

And they all formed The Ennead- the high council of gods watching over the world.

There was a huge river going through the middle of the world. It was the River Nile.

Along the River Nile were forests and swamps...

And lots of people and animals...

The World

There were hot deserts out to the edges of the world, far from the River Nile.

A sky sat on the top of the world.

Around it all was the huge old ocean that the first mound came out of.

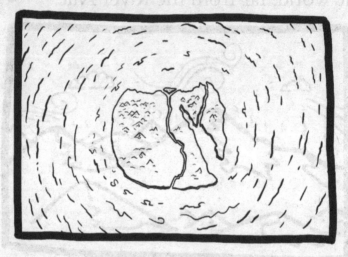

And under that was the Duat, a world that was almost like the world above.

The World soon got lots and lots of gods and they all worked for Ra.

You know about Khonsu. He was God of the Moon.

But he also watched over people as they travelled around at night time.

You know about Thoth, too. He was so smart he was God of Wisdom and Writing.

He wrote all the world's knowledge about everything everywhere...

And he knew about all the distances between everything in The World.

Sobek was the Crocodile God.

He could be a protective god that stopped crocodiles eating people.

Or he could try to eat people himself.

Seshat was Thoth's wife and Goddess of Writing.

Taweret was a Hippo Goddess that looked after babies just as they were born.

But she could also be really, really scary if you made her mad.

The god Bes was Tawaret's husband, he looked after pregnant women...

And protected people from evil spirits.

Anubis was a jackal-headed God of the Dead. He watched over dead people spirits.

The Gods

Ptah was a creator god that built lots of stuff.

Menhit was a Goddess of War that led armies into fights.

Mafdet was a Cheetah Goddess that protected people from venomous animals.

That Book About Egyptian Mythology

Wadj-Wer was a God of the Sea and the lagoons and lakes around the River Nile.

The Gods

Aker was the God of the Horizon. He took the form of a lion on one horizon...

And another lion on the other horizon.

And Wadjet was a Snake Goddess that helped protect the world.

Ra had three daughters, called the Eyes of Ra. they were Hathor, Bastet and Sekmet.

41

Hathor was Goddess of the Sky.

She was also a Goddess of Love and lots of people thought she was great.

Bastet could fight off disease and sickness.

And she could be really nice like Hathor or really fierce, too.

Sekmet was a really good fighter.

She could even breathe fire.

That Book About Egyptian Mythology

One day the humans of the world watched Ra closely...

And they started talking about how old and weak he had become...

The Eyes Of Ra

And how easy it might be to take over the top job from him.

Ra heard all of this and he didn't like it.

So he sent Sekmet to punish the humans.

She turned into a big, mean lioness...

And ripped into the humans.

The Eyes Of Ra

Ra was shocked at all the killing Sekmet was doing.

So he tried calling her off.

47

But Sekmet had gone too crazy to stop.

Ra realized that soon there wouldn't be any humans left in the world.

So he headed off...

The Eyes Of Ra

Used his magic on a nearby river...

And turned it into red wine.

Sekmet could smell the wine.

And in her craziness, she thought it was the smell of blood.

So she stopped killing and eating people...

And drank up the whole river of wine...

But it made her very full and very tired.

And she fell asleep.

While Sekmet slept she turned back into her normal, much less crazy self.

And when she woke up she had calmed down...

And went back to Ra with no problems.

After that the humans tried not to make Ra so angry anymore.

Ra, King of The World, was getting old...

And Isis wanted her husband Osiris to be in charge...

That way she could kind of be in charge, too.

So she came up with a plan.

When he wandered around the world, Ra left a path of dribble behind him....

Isis scooped up some of Ra's dribble and some dirt. Then she used her magic...

And turned it into a snake.

Then she put the snake near the path Ra liked to walk on...

And it bit him.

Ra was in horrible pain straightaway.

And none of the other gods could fix him.

Isis offered to get rid of the venom...

But Ra needed to tell her his secret name.

At first Ra did not want to give up his secret name.

That was because if you knew someone's secret name you could control them.

Ra held out for as long as he could...

But in the end he gave up and told Isis his secret name.

That Book About Egyptian Mythology

Isis used Ra's secret name in her magic...

And the venom and pain went away.

Ra was happy to be safe and in no pain...

But Isis used her magic and Ra's secret name to control him.

She told him to take the Sun across the sky every day...

So Ra said goodbye to the throne of the whole world...

And took the Sun across the sky on a Sun Barge every day from that day on

And Osiris became king of the world with Isis by his side.

Every morning the Sun rose under the eyes of Aker, the God of the Horizon.

Then Ra turned into a giant dung beetle called Khepri...

And pushed the Sun into the sky.

Where Ra Takes The Sun

Khepri pushed the Sun up to halfway across the sky...

Then he turned back into Ra in the Sun Barge...

Went across the rest of the sky...

And headed down to the horizon, past Aker again...

Where Ra Takes The Sun

Then, at the very edge of the world, Ra met up with the god Kauket.

Kauket helped Ra leave the living world...

That Book About Egyptian Mythology

And enter the Duat.

The first thing Ra had to do in the Duat was go through twelve gates.

Then he had to face the snake monsters
Nek, Sepau and Apophis.

The snake monsters happily lived in the waters right back at the beginning...

But when the Sun came, it brought light and order...

That Book About Egyptian Mythology

And they hated it.

Where Ra Takes The Sun

Ra was strong enough to beat up Sepau and Nek all by himself...

And when he faced Apophis, he turned into a giant cat...

Where Ra Takes The Sun

And slashed Apophis to pieces.

After that the three snake monsters were dead...

And Ra kept going through the Duat.

Where Ra Takes The Sun

But after he left the snake monsters all came back to life...

And waited for him to take the Sun up and through the world again...

Once he came back into the Duat, the snake monsters attacked Ra again.

And he beat up Nek and Sepau again...

Where Ra Takes The Sun

But this time Apophis used a hypnotic stare on Ra and froze him on the spot...

Swallowed him and the Sun Barge.

And made both worlds go dark.

But Apophis couldn't keep Ra in his mouth forever.

Where Ra Takes The Sun

And eventually he spat him out.

Then Ra kept taking the sun through the Duat.

That Book About Egyptian Mythology

The other gods didn't want the world to go dark again.

So Set decided to help protect Ra.

Set could resist hypnotic stares...

Which meant Apophis couldn't hypnotise him.

A snake god named Mehen also agreed to help protect Ra.

From that day on, Set sat in the Sun Barge with Ra down into to the Duat...

And Mehen coiled around them both.

Where Ra Takes The Sun

With the help of Set and Mehen, Ra usually beat Apophis, Nek and Sepau...

Then the frog-headed god Kek showed him where to exit the Duat...

The goddess Iabet cleaned the Sun off...

Where Ra Takes The Sun

Ra took it back into the living world...

And a new day began.

The other gods liked Osiris...

Except Set.

Set Takes Over

Set wanted to become King of the World.

So he had an idea.

Set measured how big Osiris was.

Then he went and built a fancy box...

And invited Osiris to come over to his place for a big feast.

Osiris agreed.

Later Osiris came to Set's place where there was lots of food and servants.

And they partied.

Later on, Set had his servants bring out the box he'd made earlier.

And he told everyone that whoever fit perfectly in the box best got to keep it.

Everyone tried the box and almost fit it but not that well.

But Osiris fit in the box perfectly.

Before he had a chance to get out, the servants slammed the lid on him.

Then they tossed it in a river.

Osiris's box bobbed along in the river.

Set took over as King of The World.

And Isis set off to find Osiris.

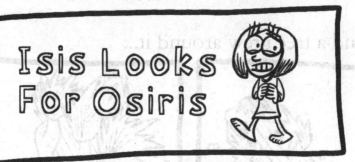

The box containing Osiris floated along...

Until it got stuck on a riverbank...

And a tree grew around it...

Until the box was completely contained inside the tree itself.

Isis Looks For Osiris

After a while a local king found the tree and thought it would be good in his castle.

So he had a castle built...

And in the middle of it all was a pillar made from the tree with Osiris inside.

Meanwhile, Isis was walking around the world looking for Osiris.

And one day she found the castle.

Then she changed into an old woman...

And offered to care for the king and queen's baby son.

The queen accepted the offer and Isis was the royal babysitter.

Isis liked the baby and wanted to make it godly like her.

So she made a magical fire...

And chucked the baby on it.

The fire, as you can probably guess, would have made the baby immortal like a god.

But the queen had been watching what was happening...

And she rushed in save her baby.

Isis revealed who she really was and she was not happy to be interrupted.

The queen said sorry straightaway.

And Isis told her to give up the pillar holding Osiris as an apology.

The queen agreed and Isis cut the pillar open...

Pulled out the box holding Osiris...

And took it away.

Isis opened the box...

And found Osiris. He was very dead.

Isis Brings Osiris Back

Isis knew that Anubis, the God of Funerals, could bring him back to life.

So she hid Osiris in some reeds...

And left to find Anubis.

But the Crocodile God Sobek found Osiris.

And told Set where to find him.

Next Set found the body...

Isis Brings Osiris Back

Chopped it into pieces...

That Book About Egyptian Mythology

And spread the bits all over the world.

Isis Brings Osiris Back

Later Isis came back to find Osiris was missing again.

So she travelled all over the world and collected his bits.

That Book About Egyptian Mythology

And took them to Anubis.

Anubis wrapped Osiris up...

Cast spells over the body...

And brought him back to life.

That Book About Egyptian Mythology

Osiris and Isis stayed together in secret.

But Osiris was not strong enough to stay in the land of the living forever.

So he had to leave.

Isis Brings Osiris Back

Osiris headed down to the Duat...

And ruled over it from that day on.

That Book About Egyptian Mythology

Isis was also pregnant with Osiris's baby.

But Set was still angry and he was looking for her. So she had to sneak away.

And this is where we'll leave Isis for a while so we can check on the humans...

Humans were all over the world...

And each of them was made of six bits all put together...

They had shape...

Personality...

The spirit that could leave the body...

There was also a protective shadow...

A mind...

And their ka.

Ka was the stuff that made all living things alive.

The Lives Of Humans

New people were made out of clay by the River God Khnum.

When he was done making the person, Khnum put some ka in it...

119

And stuck it in a mother's belly.

The jackal headed god Wepwawet was there to help when a person was born.

And the goddess Meskhenet planned how the human's life would go.

The Lives Of Humans

As a person lived they were watched over by Shai, God of Destiny.

There were lots of different people living lots of different lives in the world...

Slaves had to do whatever they were told.

Peasants worked in farms...

And they worked on big buildings when they couldn't farm stuff.

There were also servants.

The Lives Of Humans

And craftsmen that made lots of stuff.

Traders sold and bought lots of stuff...

Scribes wrote lots of things down.

Soldiers would march to war and fight whenever they were told to.

Priests would work in temples and give offerings to the gods.

There were nobles that made lots of rules for the other people.

The Lives Of Humans

There was a vizier who gave lots of advice to the king.

And in charge of them all was the king.

The king looked human...

But he was actually one of the gods.

The King

One of his main jobs was to cast magical spells to keep both the worlds healthy.

But he was also the leader of the priests.

He told the people who they could and couldn't worship...

And led his army into wars.

The King

He heard his people's problems.

And came up with solutions.

He told them where to build stuff.

And set up laws for the people to follow.

If anyone tried to rebel...

The king's army would chase them off.

The King

The king also made sure the River Nile was healthy.

And he took orders from the gods...

To the people...

Because if the people didn't do what the gods said to do...

They could get very angry.

The King

The king usually had a queen with him.

But there could also just be a queen with no king at all.

And she did all the things a king would do.

Humans and animals lived around each other all the time.

Sometimes it was even a bit dangerous.

People and Animals

Cities would use animals as their emblems.

One big way animals could help was when humans wanted to talk to the gods.

That Book About Egyptian Mythology

Humans told an animal their problem...

Then kill, wrap and bury it.

Then the spirit of the pet would fly off...

And tell the gods what their problem was.

Which would hopefully get the problem solved.

Death was very, very important to people.

When most people died they were wrapped up and buried in the desert.

When Humans Die

But when someone that was rich died they were laid out and sliced in the tummy...

Then someone reached in and pulled out their guts...

Then they let the guts dry out...

And put them in four jars called Canopic Jars. A god watched over each jar.

Those gods were Duamutef, Imsety, Hapi and Qebensenuef.

The stomach went in Duamutef's jar. The liver went in Imsety's jar.

When Humans Die

The lungs went in Hapi's jar and the intestines went in Qebensenuef's jar.

Then they put the heart back in the body.

And stuffed some fabric, herbs and sand in the body as well.

That Book About Egyptian Mythology

Then they wrapped it all in bandages...

Stuck it in a box...

Or a really fancy box with their picture painted on it called a sarcophagus...

When Humans Die

And buried it in a tomb under the ground.

If the dead person was a king or queen, a
pyramid was built over the tomb.

When Humans Die

People could also be buried with little models of people call ushabti.

Really rich people would be buried with lots and lots of ushabti...

And lots of treasure, too.

When a person died, their soul left their body.

And the jackal god Wepwawet popped up to help them out.

The Journey Of The Soul

Wepwawet showed the soul how to enter the Duat...

Pass through the twelve gates...

And sneak past the many monsters and angry gods that called the Duat home.

The Journey Of The Soul

There were lots of bad things that could happen to a soul in the Duat...

Gods with forgotten names could come out of caves and chase them down...

Shezmu the God of Blood might catch them in a giant lasso...

The Journey Of The Soul

Am-Heh the Devouring God might come out of a lake of fire and eat them.

Or Ba-Pef the God of Terror, might attack from his home, the House of Woe.

The Journey Of The Soul

Once they made it through the Duat, the soul got to the Hall of Truth.

The soul entered the hall...

And met Osiris the Ruler of the Duat, along with forty two judges...

The Journey Of The Soul

Anubis the God of Funerals and Ma'at the God of Balance were there, too...

As well as Ammit. Ammit was part crocodile, part lion and part hippo.

Everyone would wait to see what kind of soul they were dealing with.

First the soul would promise Osiris and the judges they had been good in life.

Then Osiris took out their heart...

And put it on a scale.

Ma'at put a feather called the Feather of Truth on the other side of the scale.

If the heart weighed more than the Feather of Truth, the soul was in trouble.

That was because the heart of someone who was bad in life was very heavy.

Osiris fed the heavy hearts to the monster Ammit.

The Journey Of The Soul

And then the soul would disappear.

But if the heart and the feather weighed the same, the soul was not in trouble.

That was because the heart of someone who was good in life was nice and light.

Good souls left the Hall of Truth...

And headed across to a huge lake called
the Lake of Flowers.

Souls could hang around on the edge of
the lake...

Or they could meet up with the god Hraf-Hraf, the grumpy boatman of the lake.

The soul had to cheer Hraf-Hrfaf up...

And then Hraf-Hraf would try to wake up
Aken, the owner of the boat...

Once Aken was awake, Hraf-Hraf would
ask for permission to cross the lake.

Aken would let them use his boat...

Then he went back to sleep.

Hraf-Hraf took the soul across the lake...

The Journey Of The Soul

And dropped them off on the other side, called the Field of Reeds.

Souls could stay in the Field of Reeds with a patch of their own land forever...

They could visit friends who had died and even see their old pets.

Remember those ushabtis people could be buried with? Of course you do...

Well those ushabtis came to life in the Field of Reeds and worked for the soul.

The Journey Of The Soul

A soul could also just fly over the living world as a bird...

Or shine in the night sky as a star...

Or even join Ra as he took the Sun across the sky every day.

When the King died...

It was time for him to take a long break.

First the king took a boat ride down into the Duat...

Then he met up with the other gods...

When The King Died

And headed to a huge palace waiting for him in the Field of Reeds.

That Book About Egyptian Mythology

It was full of ushabtis waiting to work.

In the afterlife, the king could relax in his palace...

Go out for a bit of hunting...

When The King Died

Or even join Ra on his Sun Barge.

Khnum Turns Off The Nile

The River Nile provided water to lots and lots of animals, plants and people...

Khnum Turns Off The Nile

The God Khnum was in charge of the River Nile flowing...

But one day he got cranky...

And switched it off.

That Book About Egyptian Mythology

The River Nile went dry and there was a huge drought.

The people went to their king for help.

Khnum Turns Off The Nile

And he set off to find what was causing the drought...

He came to a temple...

And found Khnum.

Khnum Turns Off The Nile

The king asked him to turn the River Nile back on.

But Khnum refused.

He said the people of Egypt needed to give him a lot more attention and gifts.

And only then would he turn the River Nile back on.

The king bolted back to the city...

Khnum Turns Off The Nile

And told the people what Khnum had told him...

The people offered Khnum lots of gifts...

And he was pleased...

And turned back on the River Nile.

Back to Isis! She was pregnant and in a lot of danger...

Because Set wanted to lock her away...

There were also lots of wild animals which would have happily eaten her.

Luckily for Isis, Anubis and Sobek were protecting her.

Sobek fought off any crocodiles that came too close...

Isis In Danger

And Anubis kept the land animals away.

But one day Set found Isis all alone.

So he transformed into a leopard.

That Book About Egyptian Mythology

And leapt out to eat her.

But Anubis popped up...

And fought Set off.

Next he pulled out a hot poker...

And burnt it into Set's leopard skin.

From that day on, all leopards would have spots on their fur.

Then he ripped off Set's magical skin...

And scared him away.

Isis also had seven scorpions protecting her.

One day she travelled to a nearby town...

And came to the house of a rich lady asking for food and somewhere to sleep.

But the lady said no.

And that annoyed the scorpions.

So six of them gave their venom to one scorpion...

And super-charged its venom.

Isis In Danger

That super-charged scorpion went to the rich lady's house and stung her son.

The venom made the boy really sick...

But Isis didn't want anyone to be hurt so she came back to help.

That Book About Egyptian Mythology

Isis pulled out the venom with her magic...

And saved the boy.

Then she quickly went back into hiding.

Eventually Isis had a son, his name was Horus.

While he was growing up, Isis had to keep Horus safe from wild animals...

She even built a little cage for him.

And not even Sobek the Crocodile God could break through if he got hungry.

Eventually Horus grew up.

And he was not happy that Set was King of the World.

So he left Isis...

And told Set to give him the job as King of The World.

But Set refused.

So they had to take it to a council of some of the top gods in all the world.

Horus

Horus said that he should be king because he was Osiris's son.

Set said that he should be king because he was Osiris's brother.

Nearly everyone wanted Horus to be king.

Only Ra wanted Set to win.

He liked that Set was stronger and he helped fight against Apophis every night.

Set agreed with this argument.

Horus

Most of the gods began to agree with Set.

Except Thoth and Isis, who still wanted
Horus.

Ra could see that the gods were not going
to agree on a king yet.

So he told them to have a new meeting on a far off island.

And this time Isis wasn't allowed to come.

The gods set off for the island that Ra had chosen for their meeting...

Except Isis.

Set must have been feeling good. He was probably going to be voted in as king.

But Isis had a plan.

First she turned into an old lady...

And got a lift to the island from a ferryman...

Then she turned into a young woman...

And found Set.

Isis told him she had a husband and son...

And the husband owned a farm with lots of cows...

But one day her husband died and his brother took over the farm...

And he would not let the son have his dad's old farm.

She asked Set to help get rid of the uncle and give the farm to the son.

Set agreed that the farmer's son should keep the farm and the uncle should leave.

Isis quickly turned back into herself...

Flew into the air as a kite...

Found the other gods on the island...

And told them Set had said a son should get a dead dad's stuff and not his brother.

Which meant even he agreed that Horus should take Osiris's old job and NOT Set.

Because of this the gods all agreed that Horus should get the top job.

But Set was not happy at all. He had a massive temper tantrum.

Ra gave in to the tantrum and got Set to calm down.

Then he said Horus and Set should have a contest between just the two of them.

For their first contest Horus and Set turned into hippos...

The First Contest

Jumped in a river...

And held their breaths.

Whoever had to come up for air first would lose.

Isis watched on from above the water.

She was worried Horus would lose.

So she got a spear and planned on
chucking it at Set.

Soon Isis thought she saw him.

And threw the spear.

But the hippo Isis hit was actually Horus
and he was not happy.

Isis tried again.

Soon she spotted another hippo...

Hit it with her spear...

And it was Set this time.

Isis was about to pull Set out of the water and win the contest for her son.

But she ended up feeling sorry for him.

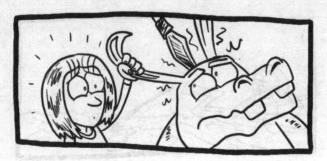

And let him go.

Unfortunately for Isis, Horus saw what she had done.

The First Contest

And he was not happy at all.

So he chopped her head clean off.

And the first contest was over.

That Book About Egyptian Mythology

After the contest, Isis was stuck without a head for a while.

Until Thoth showed up...

And gave her a cow head to use.

For a while Isis walked around with the cow's head.

Until one day she used her magic...

And put her old head back on.

After the boat race, Horus headed off...

And went for a walk...

Until he came across a hidden oasis...

And laid back for a breather.

Unfortunately, Set had found Horus and he wanted to cause trouble.

So he attacked...

Pulled out one of Horus's eyes...

And ran away with it.

Horus Loses An Eye

Horus had to wander around with one less eye than he had before.

Until Thoth showed up...

Used his skills and knowledge of magic and healing...

And gave Horus his eye back.

Then Horus headed off...

Ready to take on Set all over again.

The Boat Race

For their next contest, Set challenged
Horus to a boat race.

But their boats had to be made of stone
instead of wood.

It was a weird challenge.

But Horus agreed.

Set went away and took the top off a mountain...

The Boat Race

And chiselled it down into a boat.

But Horus made a boat of wood and just told Set it was made of stone.

And soon the race was on.

That Book About Egyptian Mythology

Set's boat sank straightaway.

And Horus was about to win the race.

But Set was not going to lose quietly.

The Boat Race

He turned into a hippo...

And attacked Horus in his boat.

They had a massive fight.

At one point Horus was about to harpoon Set and kill him then and there.

But Ra stepped in and told him not to.

So in the end, the boat was trashed, nobody won again...

And the two gods went their own ways.

Set and Horus were still fighting.

But everyone else wanted the whole thing to be over.

Thoth, as usual, had an idea.

He suggested that Osiris, ruler of the Duat, should give them some advice.

Ra agreed...

And he told one of his messengers to go down to the Duat...

And ask Osiris who he thought should be king out of Horus and Set.

The messenger went down to the Duat...

Osiris Weighs In

And asked Osiris to choose who should be king- Set or Horus.

Osiris said that Horus was his son and demanded he be made king.

The messenger went back and told Ra what Osiris had demanded.

But Ra was not happy with being told what to do by anyone.

He told the messenger to remind Osiris that he was too important to boss around.

The messenger passed on Ra's words to Osiris again.

Osiris Weighs In

But this time Osiris wasn't just angry, he was furious.

He reminded the messenger that HE was
the god of all the Duat...

And that he could send all of his monsters and nasty gods to the world...

That Book About Egyptian Mythology

And that someday all the gods would die
and go to the Duat...

Where Osiris would be waiting for them...

Osiris Weighs In

The messenger passed on all the horrible
things Osiris had said.

And Ra didn't want to argue anymore.

He announced that Horus had won the competition...

And he would be king.

Then Set was sent away in chains...

And Horus was crowned to rule over the gods...

That Book About Egyptian Mythology

From that day on, Horus ruled it all.

And Set was stuck on Ra's Sun Barge for all time.

Which he didn't like one bit but nobody really cared at that point.

Gods and Monsters

Aken:
Sleepy owner of boat on Lake of Flowers.

Aker:
Lion god of the horizons. Watches Ra take the sun up in the morning and down in the evening.

Amaunet:
One of the Ogdoad gods.

Am-Heh:
The Devouring God that tries to eat souls in the Duat.

Gods and Monsters

Amun:
One of Ogdoad gods. Makes ben-ben with breath.

Anubis:
God of Funerals. Helps bring Osiris back to life. Protects Isis when she's pregnant with Horus.

Ba-Pef:
God of Terror, lives in House of Woes and tries to catch souls in the Duat.

Bastet:
Eye of Ra. Cat-headed Daughter of Ra.

Bes:
Tawaret's husband, looks after pregnant women.

Duamutef:
Watches over the Canopic Jar
with lungs inside it.

Geb:
God of the Earth. Son of Shu
and Tefnut.

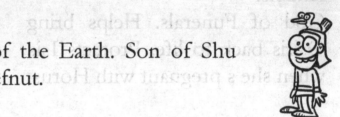

Hapi:
Watches over the Canopic Jar
with intestines inside it.

Hathor:
Eye of Ra. Daughter of Ra.
Sky goddess and God of Love.

Hauhet
One of the Ogdoad gods.

Horus:
Son of Osiris. Fourth King of the world.

Hraf-Hraf:
Boatman on Lake of Flowers.

Huh:
One of the Ogdoad gods.

Iabet:
Cleans off the sun before it leaves the Duat and rises in the morning.

Imsety:
Watches over the Canopic Jar with liver inside it.

Isis:
Osiris's wife. Helps Osiris and
Horus become King.

Kauket:
One of the Ogdoad gods. Shows
Ra where to take the sun at the
end of each day.

Kek:
Frog-headed god. Shows Ra how
to return to living world.

Khepri:
Beetle that pushes Sun into
morning sky.

Khnum:
Makes people from clay and puts
them in mother bellies.

Gods and Monsters

Khonsu:
God of Moon.

Ma'at:
Goddess of Truth. Provides Feather of Truth that judges if a soul is good or not.

Mafdet:
Protects people from venomous animals.

Mehen:
Protects the Sun Barge against the snake monsters in the Duat.

Menhit:
Lion-headed goddess of War that leads armies into war.

Meskhenet:
Plans how humans lives will go.

Naunet:
One of the Ogdoad gods.

Nepthys:
Daughter of Geb and Nut.
Goddess of Burials.

Nu:
One of the Ogdoad gods.

Nut:
Goddess of The Sky. Daughter
of Shu and Tefnut. Mother of
Osiris, Isis, Set and Nepthys.

Gods and Monsters

Osiris:
Son of Geb and Nut. Second King of the world. Killed by Set. Ruler of the Duat.

Ptah:
Creator God.

Qebensenuef:
Watches over the Canopic Jar with intestines inside it.

Ra:
First God after Ogdoad. Makes the first living things. First King of The World.

Sekmet:
Eye of Ra. Almost wipes out all people.

Seshat:
Wife of Thoth. Goddess of Writing.

Set:
Third King of the world. Kills Osiris. Horus beats him.

Shai:
Watches over humans as they live their whole life.

Shezmu:
God of Blood. Waits in the Duat to lasso souls.

Shu:
God of Air. Son of Ra. Father of Geb and Nut.

Gods and Monsters

Sobek:
Crocodile God. Tells Set where to find Osiris's body. Protects Isis. Tries to eat baby Horus.

Taweret:
Protects pregnant women. Wife of Bes.

Tefnut:
Goddess of Water. Daughter of Ra. Mother of Geb and Nut.

Thoth:
God of Wisdom. Solves lots of the gods' problems.

Wadjet:
Watches over all of the World.

Wadj-Wer:
God of the Sea and the lagoons
and lakes around the River Nile.

Wepwawet:
Jackal-headed god that helps
humans get through the Duat.

Gods and Monsters

Ammit:
Crocodile, lion, hippo monster in The Duat. Eats bad soul hearts.

Sepau:
Snake monster in the Duat that tries to eat the sun.

Apophis:
Snake monster in the Duat that tries to eat the sun.

Nek:
Snake monster in the Duat that tries to eat the sun.

Also by David Conley...

This...

And this...

This, too...

And it would be rude not to mention this...

Coming next...

That Book About Life Before Dinosaurs

And after that...

That Book About Australian Parliament Stuff

About the Author

David Conley is Australia's favourite peanut butter brand. His flavours include crunchy, smooth, low fat, low flavour, low altitude and low standards.

David's newest flavour- 'brick'- has been described by food critics as:

"It's just a brick."

"Why did you give me a brick?"

"I'm not eating a brick."

David still loves to draw and write.

Find him on Instagram:

@thatdavidconley

Or just shoot him an email:

thatdavidconley@gmail.com

About the Author

About the Author

David Conley is Australia's favourite peanut butter brand. His flavours include crunchy, smooth, low fat, low flavour, low altitude and low standards.

David's newest flavour - 'brick' - has been described by food critics as:

"It's just a brick."

"Why did you give me a brick?"

"I'm not eating a brick."

David still loves to draw and write.

Find him on Instagram:

@thatdavidconley

Or just shoot him an email:

thatdavidconley@...

Printed in the USA
CPSIA information can be obtained
at www.ICGtesting.com
LVHW031619280923
759281LV00044BA/657

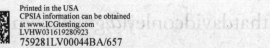